THE BUSINESS LAUNCH CODE

A Step by Step Guide
To Starting Your Own Business

M Salek

First edition - July 2018

#businesslaunchcode

www.businesslaunchcode.com

Contents

Why you need this book

Here are just a few ways this book can help you:

- Understand why new businesses fail
- Learn how NOT to fall prey to these mistakes and pitfalls
- Learn what steps you need to go through to give your business an edge
- Know who to talk to before starting your business
- Understand what qualities are important to start and grow your business
- Learn how to quickly test your idea(s) to decide if it is good or not
- Learn how to quickly determine if your business idea will be profitable
- Learn how to find out if people will buy
- Learn about the different ways to fund your business
- A quick, fun and effective way to plan your business, without spending hours!
- Learn why branding is important for a new business
- Learn about the crucial steps most new businesses miss
- Understand why it is important to take care of the small things and how this can significantly improve your business
- The 5 things you need in place to create a solid, sustainable business that won't disappear overnight
- The optimal business structure for your business
- Learn how you can get great people on board, for free
- Learn about the 3 main positions every business needs to fill
- A strategy you can use to bring down your business costs to nearly zero!
- 'Sensitivity Analysis', and why you need to know about this

- Learn about a creative strategy forf building partnerships, and how it can also help you to cut costs
- Powerful tips on how to choose a business name
- Learn how to create an effective business card
- A quick list of the records you need to keep to stay out of trouble
- 5-minute Business startup checklist, to help guide you to start your business the right way
- Learn how to make your business finally happen

And more...

This book is designed as an actionable, easy to follow, step-by-step guide - to give you what you need (and only what you need) to translate your ideas into reality.

Introduction

Most new businesses fail. That is the fact. What is unfortunate, though, is that many of those businesses could have avoided that fate had they taken care of the fundamentals before starting.

The idea for this book was born out of the desire to help people start their own businesses, while avoiding the same mistakes that cause so many to fail.

I designed the book with implementation in mind - so as to enable you, the reader, to take action and do so in a way that will take care of the important aspects as well as help you avoid the common pitfalls.

My aim is to enable you to spend no more than an hour or so on this book and gain enough knowledge to then go and decide for yourself whether your business idea is good or not. If it isn't, there's no need to despair; instead be happy in the knowledge that you have just saved yourself a lot of wasted effort, money, and heartache.

If it is a go, then you will know what you need to do next.

Reading this book won't take you long. But you will need some time (and possible re-reads) to properly understand the steps and sequence, and to grasp fully the concepts.

Before long you can actually bring to life your idea! And that is pretty phenomenal. When you do, you'll do so with the knowledge that you have already given yourself a massive edge (as opposed to most other new businesses!).

That said, there are no guarantees in life. Even the best business idea might not work out - so be prepared to be flexible. If life hands you lemons, make lemonade. But never give up.

Starting a business can be a roller-coaster ride - you will never know for certain how things will work out. But believe in your dreams, stick to your plan, be flexible, and enjoy the journey. By the end of it (if there is an end) you'll amaze yourself with all that you've achieved.

One last thing before we start: this book is not meant to be a be-all and end-all guide for you. It will provide you with **precise steps to follow**, and give you **just enough information** to take action. It will empower you by giving you only the information that you absolutely need right now (as opposed to flooding you with detail and thus cause "information overload").

There is a lot more to be learned and said about the concepts and topics covered. A whole lot more. Whole books can be written (and have been) about some of them! If you have the time available by all means go and learn more about them but realise that you **don't need to know everything**. You only need to know enough. Knowledge for the sake of knowledge can be great, but won't help you create a business, not if you don't act on the knowledge. There is a point when you need to **stop learning and start doing**.

Prioritisation is key to creating a great business. So define for yourself what is "necessary" for you - what are the things that you absolutely need to know about to make your business work? By trying to learn everything, by trying to achieve perfection, you effectively trap yourself. This is a common trap that many entrepreneurs fall into, the desire for perfection... It takes far too much energy chasing that objective. You don't need to be perfect. You just need to be good enough.

Let me ask you something - what is more important to you, making your dreams a reality or to look back 10/20 years down the line and wonder what could have been?

We entrepreneurs are a distractible bunch. Our curiousity is one of our greatest strengths, but it can also prove to be a major challenge. It is a double-edged sword. Take it from me, I know. Focusing on what you need to do now is vital to making your business a success.

So get rid of all other distractions and commit to only focusing on the task at hand, i.e. getting your business going. Do ONLY the things you really need to, and nothing more.

The book will help guide you on your journey, so that you don't have to figure it all out from scratch. But it will take work, and it's not going to be easy. All that said, it is going to be life-changing. Whether your first attempt works out or not, you will learn a lot and have a hell of a ride. It will all be worth it in the end - if you just stick with it.

I can't wait to hear of your amazing journey.

All the best!

M Salek
London, UK

How to use this book

If you are thinking of starting a Business:

Read the book from start to finish.

Use the 10 steps as a guide and follow the sequence.

Read the book at least twice. That will help solidify the steps for you. Make sure you really understand the 10 steps and what you need to do. The checklist will help.

If you are already in business:

Pick and choose chapters or sections that you feel are most relevant or important for you right now.

Set yourself a goal in terms of what it is you want to get out of that chapter, and as soon as you have understood that part / gleaned that knowledge, don't read any further. Stop, and read that again until you really understand it. Then go and apply it. After you've applied it come back and read it again - this can provide further feedback and even insights.

Once you've really mastered that aspect, then set yourself another goal, and so on...

Acronyms, abbreviations, etc

Some acronyms and other simplifications have been used in the book, where suitable (and more importantly, where I remembered!). The main ones are:

- TA = Target audience
- IC = Ideal client
- MVP = Minimum viable product
- KPI = Key performance indicator
- CRM = Customer relationship management
- BCM = Business continuity management

10 reasons why new businesses fail

On average, about 4 out of 5 new businesses in Britain don't make it to their 12th month (Source: Startup Britain). The situation isn't much different in other parts of the world.

So why is that?

Top 10 reasons why so many new businesses fail:

1. Poor management

Poor management is the top reason for most business's failure. Many business owners don't identify their gaps and don't get the help they need. This then extends to the actual management of the business as well. I have come across several businesses which were started by people who were very good at what they did, but lacked the ability to manage the business.

How The Business Launch Code addresses this: This matter is addressed in Steps 7 and 8 in particular, and the other steps also cover what those 2 steps don't.

2. Insufficient capital

A lot of new businesses run out of money, often soon after

they start, so they never even get the chance to see any results. The business owner underestimates the amount of capital required and is then forced to close.

How The Business Launch Code addresses this: This matter is addressed particularly in Step 4. Step 2 also helps.

3. Lack of planning & clear objectives

New businesses often fail to plan. Without a proper plan, it becomes quite a challenge to know where the business is going. This proves fatal for many startups.

How The Business Launch Code addresses this: Step 7, which deals with Business plans, is where this problem is addressed.

4. Poor marketing

Too many new businesses fail to put much thought into their marketing, let alone considering marketing before they start. Even if they do, they often don't commit enough resources to it. A product or service is no good if it cannot reach it's end user.

Poor marketing = poor sales = poor revenue = failed business

Enough said.

How The Business Launch Code addresses this: This matter is addressed in Step 6.

5. The business idea is not validated

I see this time and time again - a business owner sets up his business because s/he is really passionate about it, or really believes in their idea. But once they start the business they fail to generate the profit or demand required. Passion is great, but getting married to an idea usually is a recipe for disaster.

How The Business Launch Code addresses this: This is vital, and gets dealt with early on in Step 3.

6. Lack of knowledge and experience of the sector

Getting into business without proper knowledge and experience of the sector is often what causes a lot of businesses to fail.

How The Business Launch Code addresses this: This matter is addressed in Steps 1 and 8 in particular. Steps 2 and 3 will also help.

7. Failure to adapt to changes and new developments

Many businesses fail due to their inability to adapt to changes and developments in their sector/industry. Depending on the sector the business is in, the degree of importance for keeping up-to-date can vary, but it is still very important. It is particularly important if the business is in a fast-moving sector like technology.

How The Business Launch Code addresses this: This challenge is addressed in Steps 1, 7 and 8.

8. Unrealistic expectations

Unrealistic expectations is an easy pitfall for startups. When starting a business the owner gets too attached to the idea and its prospects. This leads them to create plans and projections based on faulty assumptions. A recipe for disaster that only becomes apparent when the idea is tested in the real marketplace.

How The Business Launch Code addresses this: Steps 1 and 2 deals with this issue fairly well, and step 7 also helps.

9. Poor financial management and inability to control costs

A lot of businesses fail due to poor management of their finances and their inability to control costs. Costs going out of control, poor credit control, etc. are all fairly common in new businesses.

Remember the famous business adage "Cash is King"? It is imperative to ensure that the business has a positive cashflow; but new businesses can lose sight of this crucial factor.

How The Business Launch Code addresses this: This matter is addressed in Steps 2, 7, 8 and 9.

10. Poor administration and record-keeping

Administration, boring as it may be, is important. You need to be on top of what is going on in your business - failure to do this leads to administration building up, becoming too much of a burden, and the effect can snowball (e.g. leading to poor financial practices, breach of regulatory compliance, etc.) Even though it might not be a direct factor poor record keeping can be a major reason why a business faces challenges.

How The Business Launch Code addresses this: This matter is addressed in Step 9.

How to move forward when you're unsure

The fear of failure is what holds most people back. The alternative though is what doesn't get considered - the alternative is regret, and not knowing what could have been.

Realise that nothing in life is guaranteed, nothing is without risk.

It's better to embrace your ideas and going for them than it is to look back at your life 5 or 10 years later and wonder how things could have been different.

There are a great deal of negative connotations surrounding the idea of failing - the impact of a setback is nearly always overestimated. If anything, you should dive in head-first so as to accelerate 'failure' because that is the only way you will also find the idea that will succeed.

Not every idea you have will be successful, that's just how it is. But that should not stop you from pursuing your dreams. If one way doesn't work, find another way to achieve your goals. But never stop, never give up.

No one likes to fail - but it's important to realise that a lot (if not most) of the biggest successes in the world came from failures. Be it Steve Jobs, Richard Branson, Alan Sugar... All of them have failed. But that didn't stop them, and neither should it stop you. Learn to treat failures as learning experiences. Learn from them, then move on.

I am not advocating taking unnecessary risks - far from it. Business is about minimising risk. But you do have to take some risks - it's just unavoidable. That is why I have devised this sequence of steps. They will take away and/or significantly minimise a lot of the risks associated with starting a new business, and as such help you to make your dreams come true without having to worry too much.

If you're still worried, here's something to think about - Edison failed 10,000 times before he made the electric light. If he had stopped after the first time, or even after a few hundred, he wouldn't have come up with his world-changing idea. Do not let your challenges stop you. Perseverance is a key part of starting a successful business.

Being unsure is ok, but don't let that stop you from moving forward. It is infinitely better to try and fail, than it is to do nothing.

What does being an entrepreneur really mean?

Being an entrepreneur is about having the vision and drive to push through obstacles to turn vision into reality. It's about playing many different roles, and knowing a bit about a lot of things (jack of all trade and all that).

To give you an idea, here are some of the roles of an entrepreneur:

- Visionary
- Risk taker
- Talent finder
- Manager
- Leader
- Problem solver
- Innovator

Understand that as an entrepreneur your role is not to do everything. Your job is to determine the destination and navigate your ship to reach that destination. You don't do that by doing everything - you do that by figuring out what needs to be done, what the most effective way of getting that done would be, who you need for it, and then getting those pieces of the puzzle to fit together.

You are unlikely to be an expert at any of those roles from

day one, but you will get there if you just keep at it.

Persistance really is key.

What qualifications do you need?

I've come across this question before, in one form or another.

So, what qualifications do you need - if any - to successfully start a business? Don't you need an MBA or a business degree?

Here's the simple answer - you **don't** need any qualifications!

That's right, you don't need any qualifications to start a business. Many of the most successful entrepreneurs never had any formal qualifications - you don't need any either. Will and desire counts for a lot more than any piece of paper or formal education.

If you have some sort of formal qualification that helps your idea, great. But don't feel like you can't move forward with your business idea because you don't have any qualifications.

It's your business, so you call the shots, including the requirements!

How to start a business without giving up your existing work

Starting a business does not mean you need to give up your job right away. It does help, as you can commit more time and energy to your business, but if you are really worried about not having any income while you start your business, there is a way of doing both.

Starting something on the side is an easy way to transition from working for others to running your own thing. This way you don't have much to worry about if your business idea doesn't work out, as you will have that cushion.

If you're unsure and/or worried about the whole prospect of going into business for yourself (it's quite normal, many are), this is a way to curb your fears, and start small.

Start small, take it one step at a time, and go from there. You can decide to go in full time when your business starts generating enough income for you to give up your job.

It does come at a cost however, as it can (and very likely will) slow down your progress. The more effort you put in, the faster you will move forward. That said, you get peace of mind as the upside.

Starting a business part-time gives you a taste of being an entrepreneur, but without having to worry about the risks of having no income or losing it all.

So how much time should you spend on your part time business? As much or as little as you want! Effectiveness is more important than the number of hours you spend. As the amount of time you have available is limited, always think about quality over quantity - prioritisation is key.

The one crucial thing your business must provide

When starting a new business one crucial thing a lot of entrepreneurs forget about is to focus on value and not just money.

Short-term thinking is where you only think about money, and your business's sole focus becomes generating profits.

Making money is important; after all, without money, your business won't last. But at the same time, your goal should be to provide real value to your customers. If you don't, it will become difficult to sustain the business in the long term.

The value you provide will have a direct correlation to the money you make. The more value you provide, the better your business will do.

If your goal is to create a solid, sustainable business - a business that will last a long time, a business that will endure challenges and come through stronger, a business you can be proud of - you need to focus on providing genuine value.

Create a great product or service that adds value to your customers. Something that solves a real problem, and/or something there's a real need for.

That's how you will create a great business.

The 4 main things you need before you start

Before moving on to the first step, a useful exercise is to understand what you need to create a successful business.

Here are the 4 main things you need to have:

- *Commitment:* You need to be absolutely committed to the idea. Without commitment you will lose interest as soon as you come across a challenge, and the idea dies.

- *Tenacity:* You have to have push through the challenges that get in your way. Never give up.

- *Plan:* Plan for success. Understand what needs to happen, where you are going, and how you are going there. Without a plan it becomes extremely difficult to achieve your goals.

- *Support:* Being able to ask for help when you need it is crucial to a business's success. It's impossible for a business to exist on its own, without support. This is also true when you are starting out - having support available to you will help you stay on course,

especially when the going gets rough.

If you have these 4 things in place, you can deal with whatever else comes up. No challenge can get in the way.

"You don't need to be a genius or a visionary, or even a college graduate for that matter, to be successful. You just need a framework and a dream."

Michael Dell

Step 1

Research and gather data

The path to effectively transform your idea into a real business starts with learning about your Target Audience (TA) and market. The more information you have about these, the better equipped you will be.

You need to sit down and figure out a few things, like who you are going to sell to, who your ideal customer is, etc.

You should also learn as much as possible about the market you are getting into.

Market research

The internet has made it really easy nowadays to research your market. The amount of information available at our fingertips is phenomenal. Make use of this resource to start off your research, it's certainly the easiest way to go about it. Also reference other sources like specialist magazines and newspapers, trade journals, databases, etc. (the internet might not always have all the right information).

Tip: If you're based in London (or can get to London easily) the British Library's Business and IP Centre is worth a visit. You can conduct intensive research there with free access to several specialist databases. Membership is free.

Competition analysis

Part of your research should be about identifying your competitors, and learning about them.

Here are some questions to start you off:

- Who are your competitors?
- How big are they?
- What is their business model?
- How do they market themselves?
- Which customers are they after?
- How do they reach their existing customers?
- How do they reach potential customers?

Customer profiling - What you need to know

You have to determine, even before you start, who you will

sell to. You need to know and understand your Target Audience (TA). This is THE first step to starting a business, but yet surprisingly most startups don't take this part seriously, or even consider it before getting started. Understand this - unless you know your TA you won't even be able to address their needs effectively, let alone market to them!

Here are some questions to start off your customer profiling:

- Who is buying?
- Demographic information on your ideal customer?
- Why will they buy your product or service?
- Where do they hang out? Where can they be reached?

Note: This step takes for granted that you already have a business idea. If not, or you want further information, check out the companion website.

Conclusion

It's important that you do this step diligently - it will have impact on nearly all of the other steps that follows. Without detailed information and insight about your Target Audience and market, you will be ill-equipped to formulate effective plans going forward. So don't skimp on this part. It can be somewhat tedious, but it is vital.

Note: It is important for you to realise that market research isn't a one-off thing: it needs to be an ongoing process. It might not need to be undertaken in as much detail as you do when you are doing your initial research, but you still do need to do market research from time to time. This is important because this is the only way you stay up-to-date about changes and developments in your sector, and thus be in a position to adapt to changes.

Action Steps:
1. Research your market.
2. Analyse your (potential) competitors.
3. Create a customer profile.

"Research is to see what everybody else has seen, and to think what nobody else has thought."

Albert Szent-Gryorgyi

34

Step 2

Assess your idea's potential

Your market research will set you up nicely for this second step. This step will involve a 4 stage test.

1. SWOT Analysis

2. Do the numbers work?

3. Sensitivity Analysis

4. The Smell Test

Ok, let's get started.

1. SWOT Analysis

Your research will provide an excellent basis for undertaking a SWOT analysis of your idea. Now, don't get scared by it. It is actually a fairly simple exercise, and this can prove to be an extremely useful as you evaluate the Strengths, Weaknesses, Opportunities and Threats of your idea.

Basically, all you will do is list your business idea's strengths, weaknesses, opportunities and threats.

This tool can greatly help you with the next steps. It will also give you a good idea about your idea's strengths and weaknesses.

2. Do the numbers work?

By this point in the book you should not only know details about your market and how it works, but also what your possible costs are going to be. If not, you need to devote some time to this stage and really understand whether the numbers for your business idea makes sense.

Here are the numbers you need to have:

- How much will it cost to create the product/service and deliver it to the client/customer?
- Have you factored in your own time with the costs? If not, build in how much the value of your time is going to be.
- What expenses and overheads will you have?
- How much can you sell your product and/or service for?

These are things you really need to know. This information will allow you to create a financial projection. A lot of people get scared by the prospect of creating a formal financial projection using complicated spreadsheets. But it doesn't need to be complicated at all. You can run the numbers on the back of a napkin if you wanted to. As long as you know what is involved, you're good. At the very least, you need to know how much you will need to spend (your expenses), and what you can get (your income).

The most important question you need to answer here is this: will you make more than you have to pay (i.e. bring in more money than you will have to pay out)? If yes, then go ahead to the next step. If not, work on this step to understand what you can do to improve the profitability potential, or if indeed you can do anything to improve the profitability. If not, then it perhaps is time to move on to another idea. Or, start it as a charity if you are so inclined (but that's a different path - one I'm not covering in this book).

A few tips:

- When factoring in your estimated sales, err on the side of caution. Be conservative with your expected sales figures. When you are just starting off it is very likely that you won't necessarily meet your expected sales goals, so be conservative in your plans. This way you can be prepared.

- In terms of your costs, calculate anything and everything you can think of. It's extremely important that you factor everything in, as otherwise you risk having an inflated profit figure.
- Always factor in the value of your time. If you don't do that you are effectively working for free and actually inflating your profit. That doesn't create a realistic projection of your profitability.
- Double check your numbers. Have someone else scrutinise them as well.

3. Sensitivity Analysis

Managing risk is a crucial aspect of business, and a sensitivity analysis can help you with that quite significantly. This part is about understanding the uncertainties that cané affect your business (like seasons, trends, etc), and creating a game plan to deal with them.

Every business has some variables and uncertainties that need to be considered to realistically determine its chances of success.

Sensitivities need to be understood and factored in. Variables like this need to be understood to get a real picture of the potential of your idea. For example, if your business doesn't operate for one month in the year (for whatever reason), your projection should be based on the turnover for 11 months. So find out what sensitivities can impact your business, and how you can deal with them.

Examples of sensitivities may include:

- Seasonality
- Staff retention and turnover rate
- Staff holidays
- Discounts provided (for products / services)
- Trends
- Geo-economical factors

4. The Smell Test

As one of my favourite entrepreneurs, James Caan, puts it this is about finding the critical element in your business that can make or break it.

This is important.

So determine: what is the most critical element for your business?

What will happen if you don't have that in place? What

options do you have to get it in place (if you don't already)? Do you need to protect this critical element?

Take some time and really think about this. This can make or break your business.

Conclusion

At the end of the day, all you are doing at this stage is determining what is going out and what is coming in. If you have more coming in than going out, then you are going to be profitable. If not, then you need to rethink your strategy.

The question you need to have answered at this stage is whether there is enough money in it for you.

Is there?

If not, why would you want to go ahead with this business idea?

Action Steps:
   1. Do a SWOT analysis of your business idea.
   2. Determine if your numbers work.
   3. Do a Sensitivity analysis of your idea.
   4. Do a Smell test of your idea.

"Even if you don't have the perfect idea to begin with, you can likely adapt."

Victoria Ransom

Step 3

Validate your idea

By now you should know your market, and understand the numbers and sensitivities. That should give you a fair amount of confidence in your concept. It is at this stage you will test the idea to see if it really holds water or not.

This will start with a 2 stage validation test. I've created a 2 stage test so that you can be as thorough as you need to be. For instance, often just Stage 1 will be enough to decide if the idea is worth pursuing or not. That way you won't need any more time or effort to be spent on the matter. If an idea is a no-go, it is better to find out sooner than later.

Ok, now let's explore the 2 stage test.

The 2 stage Validation Test

Stage 1 will help you to quickly determine the potential of your business idea. Some of the questions here will be repeating points covered in the earlier steps. This is deliberate - I want you to be absolutely sure about these questions.

Stage 2 will be more extensive, and usually involve contact with your potential buyers.

Stage 1 - Quick self test

Ask yourself these questions:

1. Is there a market for your idea?

You won't know for certain if there is a market for your idea (until you actually put the product/service out there), but this will be part of your market research. The point of this question is to quickly check if there is a possible need for your product or service. If there isn't any evident demand, it will be more difficult for you to validate the idea (not to mention risky).

2. Are you the right person for this venture?

Realise what your business will involve, and ask yourself if you are the right person or not for this business. For example, if you are starting a financial services firm but don't like number-crunching, then perhaps you are not the best person for this venture. That doesn't mean though that you shouldn't go ahead with it - especially if it is a good idea. All it means is that you'd be better off finding someone else who is suitable for carrying on the aspect of the business which doesn't fit your personality or preferences. That way you can still run the business and enjoy its success, without being tied down by something that you don't want or like.

3. Does the pricing make sense?

Easiest way to find out is by finding out how much your competitors are charging. If your prices are about the same, then you can't go far wrong... Then consider what it actually will cost you to deliver that product or service. If selling at the market price leaves you with an acceptable level of margin, then it is an idea that you can move ahead with. But if the numbers don't make sense, then it's unlikely that this venture will be a profitable one. You are better off finding something else that actually will work.

4. Do you know your market?

Research can prove to be vital for you, not just at the inception, but in long-term too. So start off on a strong footing, and really learn about your market. The more information you have about your market, the better position you will be in.

5. Do you have the tenacity and desire to see it through?

It won't be smooth-sailing - creating a successful business takes work. There will be bumps along the way, so you have to be willing to work through them. Determination is a vital entrepreneurial skill.

6. Does your idea withstand the "stress test"?

Find holes in your idea - ask why or for what reasons your business could fail. If possible, involve others in the process (really useful if you can get feedback from experts in your industry). The sole objective of this test is to find reasons why your idea might not work. This way you will find out about potential problems without actually stumbling across them the hard way, and then work on finding solutions before they occur. Even if you find that there are no solutions available, that is still a great result, as you've just saved yourself a lot of wasted time and resources! The information you gain from this test can help you avoid serious problems in the future.

If you have said 'Yes' to all 6 of the above questions, then move on to Stage 2, i.e. validation.

Stage 2 - Validation

In stage 2 the idea is to find out, as soon as possible and with as little investment as possible, whether the idea you have will work. Stage 1 already involved some work towards validating your idea, Stage 2 takies it further.

There are various methods of validating an idea, and the best method(s) for validating your idea will really depend on what you are selling. The next section will go through 5 ways you can validate your ideas.

Case Study on Validation (and why it is important)

Zappos is a great model to cite here. Before spending a lot of time and money on their business, they wanted to determine if people would actually spend money on buying shoes online (this was in the early 1990s). So they quickly put together a website, with images from manufacturer's websites. When they started getting sales, they would go to the nearest shoe store, buy the shoe in question at full retail price and ship it to the customer. They did lose some money on each pair sold, but it provided them with valuable feedback - they knew that their business idea was a potentially viable one. This is what you need to do as well.

Move fast, quickly and inexpensively validate your business idea, and move forward only if the idea is validated. This is a great way of reducing your risks.

5 Quick Validation techniques

Here are five ways you can quickly and effectively validate your business idea:

1. *Phone calls* - Pick up the phone and talk to 10 or more of your prospective clients. This is a great way of validating your idea. If your idea is indeed something that there is a demand for, you might actually end up with some paying clients using this method.

2. *Google Ads* - Google ads are the small ads you see when you search for something on google. This can be a great way to test your idea by factoring in the response and actions your ad generates. A quick way to use this method would be to put together an ad for your website (you can quickly put together one if you don't have a website for the product or service) and then setting up a small campaign with Google Ads. You can test this on other platforms as well, eg. Facebook.

3. Classifieds - You can easily create a small classified ad targeting your potential customer (or client) in a newspaper or magazine they read. There are online classified sites as well which can be useful, like Loot.com or Gumtree.com.

4. Market stalls - This can be a great way of testing demand for a product. The idea is to hire a stall at a market where your Target audience goes to, and then gauge the response. You can even generate some sales while having the opportunity to interact with your TA. That alone can be worth the expense as it can provide you with invaluable feedback.

5. Leaflets - The idea with this is to design a leaflet (it doesn't need to be anything award-winning, just create one on Word or Canva - you can even get free templates). Then distribute it where it will reach your TA. Then wait for the calls or emails. How long a wait is reasonable will depend on your product/service, but I'd say a week is a reasonable period of time.

By the way, if your business idea involves a physical product you really don't need a stockpile of them. Even just the concept and particulars can usually be enough for you to validate the idea and its potential (see the Zappos example in the last section). It can also be useful to check out how other product developers/entrepreneurs are doing it on places like Kickstarter, to get ideas.

Action Steps:
1. Go through stage 1 of the 2-stage Validation test.
2. Go through stage 2 of the 2-stage Validation test (use the 5 validation techniques to help with this).

"Don't worry about funding if you don't need it. Today it's cheaper to start a business than ever."

Noah Everett

Step 4

Fund your business

Considering how you are going to fund your business is an extremely important piece of the puzzle. A lot of new businesses fail due to the insufficient capital - you don't want to find yourself in that position. Avoid it by planning it in advance.

The 3 main ways to fund your business:

Broadly speaking, there are 3 main funding routes for you: Bootstrapping, Borrowing, and Equity Share. I'll cover each of these briefly below:

Bootstrapping - The idea of bootstrapping is to run your business using the least amount of financial resources possible. Basically, you will be self-funding, if you are funding at all that is. Bootstrapping does require a lot of creativity in terms of finding alternative solutions and maximising what you have. It can be a really useful exercise, to bootstrap your business to start with (as opposed to seeking investment right away), because it forces you to learn every part of your business and to ensure everything works as efficiently as possible. This way, further down the line when you do take on investment, you will maximise its utilisation (and ROI).

Borrowing - There can be several sources from which you can borrow money. The easiest source would be friends and family, while the more formal route would be a bank. Crowdfunding is yet another source of borrowing money, and perhaps one of the best ways these days.

Equity Share - This is the domain of Private equity, the idea being that you give away part of your business in exchange for investment. This is where Angel Investors and Venture Capitalists come in. If you're interested in this route, check out the companion website for resources on getting angel investment; and VC funding.

How you can bring your costs down to nearly Zero

Freesourcing is a strategy which can help you to bring your costs down significantly. This is a concept you should definitely become familiar with, especially if you choose to bootstrap your startup.

The basic idea here is to "freesource" as many of the resources you need as possible, i.e. find free alternatives of the things you need. You will be surprised how many times you can actually find a free alternative. All you need to do is look, and be creative.

Thinking out of the box is a valuable resource for entrepreneurs.

There's a whole book on this topic - check it out to learn more: Freesourcing by Jonathan Yates.

A creative way to create partnerships & cut costs

Yet another strategy that can help you massively is Bartering. Bartering can be a great way of cutting your costs and creating great partnerships at the same time. It can help you no matter what stage of growth your business is in, so it is definitely a concept worth adopting.

Here's a great example of how bartering works: Hotels have unused rooms all the time. The same is true for Airlines, who usually don't have 100% uptake. So most of the big hotels and airlines have partnerships which basically allow Airlines staff to get free rooms, and in exchange the hotel staff get free tickets with the Airlines.

Do you see how they utilised unused resources to cut their costs and create a great partnership? How can you use bartering in your business?

Conclusion

The main question you need to answer in this step are these: how are you going to fund your business? Are you going to be funding it yourself? Will you need outside help?

Note: For further help with this step, check out the companion website.

Action Steps:

1. Determine the amount of money you will need to create and run your business.
2. Determine how you will fund your business.

"Always deliver more than expected"

Larry Page

Step 5

Determine your business's identity

This step is about branding, and determining your business's identity. A lot of new businesses think that branding is just for large businesses. Nothing could be further from the truth. The very fact that you exist and people know you means you have a brand, so you might as well make effective use of it.

Having a strong brand is a great way of having an edge over your competitors, and also makes it easier to acquire and retain clients.

The starting point (in terms of branding) for a new business is the name, of course. The logo can be dealt with after that. Do realise, however, that branding isn't just about the name or the logo - it's your business's identity. As such it's about the impression the business conveys to its end users and stakeholders. This is yet another reason why Customer service is so important. Managing your business's reputation is a crucial aspect of branding.

Business name

When starting a new business having a good name can help build your presence. It's not the be all and end all by any means, but it's all about giving you the best chances to succeed.

Here are some tips on choosing a business name:

1. Think what sort of name will resonate with your TA. Your market research will prove to be very useful here as you can determine how relevant any name idea you come up with will be with the information you have about your TA. Ask yourself - how would it make your Target Audience feel? What will they think when they hear your business's name?

2. Check on your competitors. What sort of names do they have? You can use those to spark off your own ideas.

3. Consider how your business name will make your partners, employees, suppliers, etc. think and feel.

4. Visualise the name, and determine how it makes you feel and think.

5. Take into account all possible connotations that your

business name may have. You don't want to have a name which might actually be offensive to a potential overseas client because it means something bad in their language! Of course it's not practical to expect you to go through translating the potential name in every language available, but think about the major languages especially if it's a one-word name.

6. Don't be too specialised. For example if you are starting off a business to offer Bookkeeping services, it still might be better not to name it XYZ Bookkeeping services. When your business grows, which may involve offering other services too down the line, you don't want your name limiting you.

7. Get feedback from friends, family, potential clients, and people in the same industry, etc. Factor in that feedback and suggestions about the impression they have of your name ideas to decide on your business's name.

8. Keep it short.

9. When you do settle on a name, give it some time to turn-over in your mind. Sleep on it. If you still feel good about it the next day, then go for it.

Business logo

Your business's logo should be something that is not completely irrelevant. If your Target Audience is a conservative bunch, making your logo really loud, colourful, etc doesn't make much sense...

Depending on your budget and time availability, in the initial stage even a draft will do. You can always improve on it, even change it, after you generate some income. But you really can create one fairly simply these days, using online tools like Canva.

If you are interested in creating your own logo, check out the additional resources on the companion website: www.BusinessLaunchCode.com

Business card

Having a business card is useful, but don't spend too much time on it. As long as it is a standard format, and provides the message, you are good. Go for something simple and effective.

Saying that, I'd recommend having business cards only if you plan on doing a lot of face-to-face meetings etc.

Otherwise it's unlikely they'll be of much use. Business cards are not nearly as important as they used to be.

So, create a business card if it is important for your business. You can hire someone on fiverr.com to design this as well. Or, you can use one of the many online business card printers to create one yourself - you can use their online tools and then have it printed.

Check out the next section for more tips on this, namely the 3 main things you need in a business card to make it truly effective.

How to create an effective business card

The business card is there to quickly remind (and inform) others about the crucial elements of your offering. The 3 most important things your card should have are:

1. Your Unique Selling Point (USP).

2. A catchy message informing how you / your business can help, and what you offer.

3. How they can contact you.

As long as you have at least these three elements on your card, you have an effective business card.

Don't complicate it - simple is good.

Conclusion

Think about your business's identity and what impression you want your business to convey. Then determine how best to convey that via things like your business name, logo, business card, etc.

Action Steps:

1. Finalise the business name.
2. Find a suitable domain name.
3. Create a logo.
4. Decide if having a Business card is actually going to help.
5. Create a business card, if it is important for your business.

"A brand is the set of expectations, memories, stories and relationships that, taken together, account for a consumer's decision to choose one product or service over another."

Seth Godin

Step 6

Reach your Target audience

You will have a fair amount of information and insight about your business by this stage, which will be crucial when planning how to reach your potential customer (or client). Without an effective strategy, it will be difficult for you to reach your TA, which in turn limits your abilitiy to generate any revenue. So you really do need to get this part dealt with.

The work that you did in the first step will be vital here, as you will be using the information and insights gained about your Target Audience (and market) to create a plan that will be effective for your business.

Marketing Strategy

Here are some questions which can help you create a marketing strategy.

- How are you going to reach your clients?

- What is your value proposition?

- How are you going to get new customers? What is your customer acquisition strategy?

- What is your Elevator pitch (i.e. a sales pitch you could deliver in just a couple of minutes)?

- What is your Unique Selling Point (USP)?

If you want more help with this, check out the One page marketing plan template on the companion website: BusinessLaunchCode.com

Marketing mix

There are many ways to reach your Target Audience. An effective marketing strategy will consist of not just one of these mediums, but several of them. Marketing mix is basically about determining what marketing channels and activities you should use. Marketing strategy determines how to use them. So in this stage, give some thought to all the different ways you can reach your Target Audience, as well as how they can fit together. This is something you need to keep in mind while developing your marketing and sales strategy.

Digital marketing

Having an online presence is critical these days. At the very least, you need to have a website. Depending on the sector you are in and where your Target Audience hangs out, you might also need to have a presence in the other Social media channels like Facebook, Twitter, etc.

Tip: No matter which sector you are in, consider having a presence on Youtube. This is one of the main places people look for information these days.

Sales Strategy

Having a clear strategy for every part of your business will give you a massive edge (not to mention the time and effort you will save). This includes sales - even if you skip having a clear strategy for some of the other parts, you should definitely not skip sales.

Ideally, you need to determine your sales strategy, as well as your sales funnel, to plan how your product or service will be sold.

Here are some questions to get you thinking about it:

- How are you going to sell to your customer? What is

your sales strategy?

- How are you going to retain your customers?

- How will you ensure that your Customer Service is exceptional?

- How much will it cost you to acquire a client (Client acquisition cost)?

Sales is one of the most important parts of creating a successful business - without selling, your business will never generate any income. Without income, it will not be a successful business.

Business networking

When it comes to reaching your TA and spreading the word, networking can hardly be ignored. It is especially useful if you are bootstrapping your business.

There are many advantages to networking, but only if done effectively.

Here are five essentials to keep in mind when deciding on your networking strategy:

1. Be selective - When it comes to choosing networking

events, choose the ones where you can help and add value, and the attendees can potentially do the same for you.

2. *Keep your eyes and ears open* - Networking doesn't just happen in formal networking meets and events, they can happen in any setting. Any place where you meet others can provide potential to network. Keep your eyes and ears open, that is how you will find opportunities in everyday situations.

3. *Add value* - Go to a networking meet with a genuine intention of adding value, and helping others. Don't be selfish. Give before you ask.

4. *Connect* - Don't be one of those people who attends events to simply spread their business cards around. No one cares about that style of networking. Genuinely connect with people.

5. *Follow up* - One of the biggest mistakes people make in terms of networking is not following up. Always follow up.

Conclusion

Having an effective marketing strategy is vital to the success of your business. It can literally make or break your idea! So make sure you spend some time and effort to get this part right.

However, don't think that you will need to spend a lot of money to have an effective marketing strategy - be creative! Think how you can reach your Target Audience without spending a lot.

Action Steps:
1. Create a marketing plan.
2. Create a networking strategy.
3. Determine your sales funnel.
4. Develop a sales strategy.

"The price of success is hard work, dedication to the job at hand, and the determination that whether we win or lose, we have applied the best of ourselves to the task at hand."

Vince Lombardi

Step 7

Plan for success

Now that you have done your research, validated your idea, and determined how you're going to reach your customer, it's time to create a plan for your business.

Let me start off by saying that a business plan isn't really as complicated as a lot of entrepreneurs think. Although there are set templates and standards which are expected by organisations like Banks when applying for loans, that is not what you really need here. The objective for Step 7 is to clearly define (for yourself and your business partners, if applicable) what you intend to achieve. What are your goals for the business?

Your business plan doesn't need to be an overly complicated document with pages and pages of information. You can have something really simple - it doesn't need to be more than a page - but you really should have a plan. A plan is important: unless you have a clear idea about what you want to do and where you want to go, keeping yourself on track will be difficult.

Be flexible and change your business plan as things change, but at least have a guideline. This will help you to stay on course.

Why having a Business plan is important

So why do you need a Business plan? Here are 5 reasons:

1. To plan the future of your business, and thus provide you with a clear plan of where it's heading.

2. To help the business grow.

3. To help secure funding.

4. To help know what comes next.

5. To help plan and manage finances.

The essential elements of a Business plan

The essential elements your business plan should include are as follows:

- Goals
- Requirements
- Potential challenges and solutions
- Financial projections

- Competition analysis
- Marketing and sales strategy
- Budget
- Growth strategy

Quick business plan hack (quick and fun business planning)

One way of doing a quick business plan is to use the Business Canvas. It provides you with a quick snapshot of the important aspects of your business. Have a go at it and see what you think. You can find more details, as well as a template for the Business Canvas, at the companion website: BusinessLaunchCode.com

Conclusion

A lack of plan is what causes a lot of new businesses to fail. By going through this step now you can save yourself a lot of headaches down the line.

It really is as the saying goes "If you fail to plan, you plan to fail." So don't fail to plan!

Action Step:

1. Create a business plan, and/or business canvas.

Yes, there is only one thing to do for this step, but it's an important one, so avoid the temptation to skip this part.

"Your brand is what other people say about you when you're not in the room"

Jeff Bezos

Step 8

Plug the holes

When starting off, two very important questions to ask yourself are:

1. What skill sets and experience will be required to run your business successfully, and
2. How many of them you yourself have.

It is very likely that there will be areas of the business where you are not the greatest - sales, for example, might not be something you want to do. So that would be one task you should find someone else to take on. It's all a matter of finding people who will plug those holes for you, and in the process, make your business more robust.

Doing everything on your own - marketing, finance, sales, operation, etc. - is not easy, nor practical. Managing all the different aspects of a business by yourself can actually be suicidal for the business as it takes you away from what you are really good at.

Ideally, you should be focusing on your strengths and find

people who are good at the other parts to take care of the rest. If you are truly multi-talented, then great. But even then life will be a lot easier if you have help.

Take into account the fact that you are only one person, and there are only 24 hours in a day.

Start alone if you have to, but delegate as soon as you can.

On that note, if you need help identifying your strengths (or weaknesses), check out this book: StrengthsFinder 2.0. The test that comes with the book is widely considered the best tool for determining your strengths and weaknesses. Can be very insightful, especially when you are starting off.

Advantages of <u>NOT</u> doing it alone

1. You can feed off the motivation of others: Keeping yourself motivated often becomes a challenge, especially if there is no one else to share the journey with. Having other people on board makes the business idea more real, and their motivation can actually help you to motivate yourself, especially when you feel disillusioned (and trust me, you will have those moments). This is one of the biggest advantages of not doing it alone.

2. You can complement your skills with those you are lacking: As mentioned before, you are unlikely to possess all the required skills and experience. Having others on board who do helps you to effectively fill any gaps.

3. It frees up your time to do the things you do well and enjoy: By not having to do everything on your own, you can focus on the things you are good at, and/or really enjoy doing. This way you also eliminate the risk of the business becoming a chore.

4. It frees up your time to grow and scale your business: Having other people share in the responsibilities of the business means you can actually focus your time on growing your business.

5. Two heads are better than one!: No matter how good you are at coming up with ideas and solutions, it is always better to have others providing feedback. You can get alternative solutions, and brainstorming can spark ideas which otherwise you wouldn't have had.

6. You can share the risk: If you have team-members who are partners then you will be sharing the risk of the business with them.

7. You can face challenges together as opposed to facing them alone: As they say, there is strength in unity. You will be in a stronger position to face challenges when doing it with your team, as opposed to doing it all by yourself.

3 main positions every business needs to fill

At the very least, every business should have 3 main roles that needs to be filled –

3. Operations - someone who is going to manage the business, and execute and deliver the product and/or service

1. Marketing & Sales - someone who is going to manage the marketing and do the selling (further down the line, when your business starts taking off, consider getting specialists for marketing and sales, and splitting this into 2 roles).

2. Finance - someone who is going to deal with the finances of the business.

In many cases you can manage 2 of those functions yourself, or find someone who can do the same, but managing all 3 roles becomes a challenging task.

If your business is technology based, then you will also need someone to manage that.

A creative way of finding potential partners, and talent, for free!

A great way of filling the gaps in your business and finding potential partners is to find Co-founders.

The idea is a simple one – you find people who possess the skillsets and/or experience that you absolutely need but don't have, and make them a partner.

The concept of having co-founders seems like a fairly new one, but actually it has existed for as long entrepreneurship. Very few of the most successful ventures were started by one single person. Apple was the work of Steve Jobs and Steve Wozniak, Microsoft was Bill Gates and Paul Allen, Berkshire Hathaway became tremendously successful under Warren Buffet but Charlie Munger played an integral part in it, and the list goes on and on.

Of course, if you already have someone that you like, and/or want to work with, then this piece of the puzzle is solved for you. If not, or if you still have gaps in your business that you need to fill, then finding a co-founder can be a good option, especially if you are not in a position to hire someone yet.

There are several places you can go to, like Meetup.com, which has groups of like-minded individuals who can be ideal as co-founders. Also check out local networking clubs and meetings, industry-specific events and of course, word of mouth.

Conclusion

Whether you hire or take on partners, make sure that they are the right people. Spending some time in the beginning ensuring this will save you a lot of trouble later on.

As an entrepreneur, your job isn't to do everything. It is far better to find someone else who can do the job well. Anytime you find a gap or require a particular skill set or knowledge, ask not how you can learn it yourself. A better question to ask is who you can find to do that task for you.

Understand the value of bringing in the skills you lack - the sooner you plug the holes in your boat, the smoother the ride will be.

Action Steps:

1. List your strengths and weaknesses (use a test like the one in StrengthsFinder if that helps).
2. Determine the gaps, and how you will fill them.
3. Determine how you are going to fill the 3 main positions.
4. Decide if you want/need a partner.

"You can't connect the dots looking forward; you can only connect them looking backwards. So you have to trust that the dots will somehow connect in your future. You have to trust in something – your gut, destiny, life, karma, whatever."

Steve Jobs

Step 9

Put the other pieces in place

This step is about getting an edge, and making sure that the smaller pieces are also in place.

Here are the 5 things you need in place to ensure your business runs smoothly, and continues to grow:

1. Administration
2. Systems
3. CRM
4. KPIs
5. BCM

Having these parts in place will ensure that your business will run smoothly, and will continue to grow. These 5 things won't only help you run your business for smoothly and effectively, they will also eliminate a lot of unimportant stuff that will inevitably crop up down the line, and keep things simple and straightforward. Makes for much less stress and headaches.

Note: You can work on them as you continue to build your

business - they are not essential from day one. But do make sure that you have them in place as soon as possible, preferably in the first 3 months of starting your business.

Administration

Take care of all the administrative stuff and record-keeping. Create systems to ensure that the things that are essential are recorded without a hitch. For example, things like Annual Returns and Tax returns should never be delayed. So put in place reminders on your Calendar or your Customer Management System (CMS).

Determine what policies you need to have in place (e.g. Health and Safety, Quality management, Employee Handbook), then have them in place.

The idea here is to ensure that whatever record you need to keep you are recording, and whatever rules and policies you need to comply with you are complying with.

Here's a quick list of the information you absolutely should record, and the policies you ideally need to have:

- Annual Returns
- Tax Returns

- VAT Returns (if you need to be VAT registered)
- Health and Safety policy
- Employee Handbook
- Employee records

Depending on the sector you are in, or even where you are based, you might have different record-keeping and regulatory requirements. Consult your local Chamber of Commerce or the relevant government agency for further information.

Note: If you are starting off on your own (one man operation), and don't/won't have any employees any time soon, you can delay working on the policy elements. But do get those in place as soon as you start bringing employees on board.

Systems

You will make your life and business much simpler once you systemise your business.

Understand this - you are running a business, not a hobby. Unless you systemise your business, you will be running it inefficiently, and waste a lot of time, effort and, financial resources. The hours you spend repeating a process are hours you can spend on more valuable tasks, like talking with prospective clients and securing new business.

Once you've achieved this, you will find yourself in a position to go and grow your business a lot faster and without a lot less headaches.

Growing a business 'organically' can be an interesting ride, but in my experience, having gone through that process, I also know what a difference it would have made to have the business systemised from the beginning. Conversely, it was also when I had systemised parts of a business that I saw the most amount of difference, especially when it became evident that had I not done so I would have ended up repeating things and wasting time and effort.

I'm a big fan of efficiency. I don't like wasting my time and resources, neither should you. You are in business now - carefully allocate your resources (especially time).

CRM

CRM (Customer Relationship Management) systems are basically software systems that help you to record what is going on in your business and streamline the process. A CRM can prove to be of great help to a business, especially once you start growing. It can significantly improve the way you retain information and communicate internally, as well as with clients, and also help to systemise the business.

I wouldn't recommend spending a lot of money on an expensive CRM solution, and most definitely not when you are just starting off. You can "freesource" one - it doesn't make sense to spend money that'll be much better spent elsewhere. There are several free CRMs which do a decent job. So try them out first.

If, down the line, you need a more feature-packed CRM you can look into the paid-ones. But I'd recommend doing that only when your business can justify the expense (granted of course that the solution does offer significant benefits).

Here are some free CRMs you can try out:
- Zoho CRM
- HubSpot CRM
- Insightly
- Zurmo
- SugarCRM

KPIs

KPIs stand for Key Performance Indicators. These are metrics you can use to measure the performance of your business. It is important to incorporate ways of measuring the performance of your business. At the end of the day if you don't measure how your business is performing, you won't know what to improve, or even what is under-performing.

Depending on your business what you need to measure will vary. But here are some general ones to spark off your own ideas:

- Conversion rate
- Revenue Growth Rate
- Gross Profit Margin
- Net Profit Margin
- Customer Lifetime Value
- Sales per channel

BCM

A BCM (Business Continuity Management) plan is something I would recommend every business to have in place. Basically, it's planning for risks and problems, this is about having a contingency plan.

Also known as a BC (Business continuity) plan, it's like insurance - you should always have a plan for the worst-case scenario, so that if something does go wrong you will be prepared for it. It's impossible to predict every possible challenge, but not preparing at all leaves you far more vulnerable than preparing for those you can think of.

Creating a BCM will involve things like planning your backup, planning ways of securing your business against accidents, etc.

Most businesses overlook or ignore this (intentionally, or unintentionally) - try not to do that. By doing this, you plan to live another day. So definitely something you should undertake, and do so seriously, and not just as an administrative exercise.

Conclusion

Taking care of the administration of the business, and systemising it, will not only help you cut down on problems in the future, it will also help you to grow.

Understand the concept of "Opportunity cost" and internalise it - it will transform the way you think about business, and

Understand what it means to systemise, and how it can help you. Communicate this to your team as well. Initially this step might seem a bit tedious, but this will pay off down the line. You'll thank me then even if you don't now!

Action Steps:

1. Understand the 5 things you need in place to ensure your business runs smoothly, and continues to grow.
2. Determine how you will take care of the administrative stuff and record-keeping.
3. Think about ways you can systemise your business.
4. Determine if having a CRM can be useful (and if so, which one).
5. Determine your main KPIs.
6. Create a BCM plan.

"Focus on small successes along the way to help you achieve your goal sooner."

Joy Mangano

Step 10

Structure and formalise your business

The last step is where you formalise your idea - the nine steps leading up to here were there to build up your idea, test it, and have the things you need in place to make sure that the business is sustainable. They are everything you need to create a viable, solid business. If you have come this far then it probably makes sense to go ahead and formalise your business.

Saying that, if you haven't gone through the previous steps, formalising is pointless.

Note: What legal structure will be best for your company will be something you'll need to discuss with a professional in your country or region. I'm most familiar with the process in the UK, so what follows will be information as per the UK business structures and methods of incorporation. If you are not in the UK, consult your local Chamber of Commerce or relevant government body.

I've divided this part into 2 sections - the first deals with the business structure, and the second with incorporation.

1. Business structure – determine which will be suitable for you

There are the 3 main business structures which your business will fall under:

Sole Proprietorship: This is basically where you run your solo-show. No employees and no formal structure. All you do is inform the HMRC about being self-employed, because that is effectively what you are when you are self-employed. If you feel that this is the right option for you, it might still be worth having a chat with your local tax office about this matter.

Limited Company: This is the most common structure for startups. You register a company, and this limits your liability. With this structure you are never personally liable for anything, which is one of the biggest advantages of registering as a limited business.

Partnership: Pretty self-explanatory – this is the structure you go for when you have partners. You'll usually be going for a Limited company structure, having multiple shareholders, or the LLP structure.

If you have further questions about business structure, contact the relevant goverment department in your country (eg. Companies House in the UK, SBA in USA), and/or your local Chamber of Commerce.

Different coutries will have different rules and processes, but by and large the 3 above are the main structures, even if the names vary.

2. Incorporation

If you have decided to form a Limited company or a Limited Liability Partnership, then you go through the stages of incorporation.The relevant government department of your country (eg. Companies House in the UK, SBA in USA) will have all the details you need, so check out their website for more information.

The steps to incorporate your business is usually fairly straight-forward, so you should be able to take care of it yourself. If you are uncertain about something, call up your relevant government department - they'll be more than happy to help.

Action Steps:

1. Decide on the legal structure of your business.
2. Determine the process for incorporating your business.
3. Incorporate!

"You miss 100 percent of the shots you don't take."

Wayne Gretzky

Next steps

If you are here (and have followed the steps sequentially), then you have gone through all the steps. Congratulations! Now you are in a position to go ahead and start assessing your idea and determine it's chances of being more than just an idea. Below is a handy checklist to help with this.

5 Minute Business Startup Checklist

Here's a quick checklist to help start your business.

1. Have I researched my sector and/or market? Do I know about my customers, their needs, wants, etc? (Step 1)

2. Do I know who my TA is? (Step 1)

3. Do the numbers work? (Step 2)

4. Have I validated my idea? Is there potential? (Steps 2 & 3)

5. Have I determined the capital needs and how I will fund the business? (Step 4)

6. Have I determined my business's identity? (Step 5)

7. Do I have a marketing plan? Do I know how my product/service will reach the customer? (Step 6)

8. Do I have a sales strategy? Do I have a plan for selling my product/service? (Step 6)

9. Do I have a business plan? Do I know where my business is going and how it will get there? (Step 7)

10. Do I have the right people on board? (Step 8)

11. Have I put in place the small things that will ensure smooth-running in the long-term? Have I systemised the busines (if not, do I know how I can)? (Step 9)

12. Have I decided on my business structure? Will it be incorporated? (Step 10)

10 Pitfalls to avoid, and how to avoid them

Let's take on board the major reasons most startups fail, and how you can avoid them. This should act as a quick summary of the 10 major pitfalls, and how the Business Launch Code helps you to avoid them.

1. *Poor management:* You can avoid this trap by ensuring that you have the right people on board, and have a clear plan.

2. *Insufficient capital:* Thinking through your numbers and how you are going to fund your business will help you to avoid this challenge.

3. *Lack of planning.* Creating a clear business plan will help you to deal with the risks posed by lack of planning.

4. *Poor marketing:* Step 6 - which is where you create a marketing plan - should prevent this issue from arising in your business.

5. *Idea not validated:* The validation stage (Step 3) deals with this.

6. *Lack of knowledge and experience of the sector:* By and large you can negate this as an issue by

undertaking market research and really learning about your market. Having the right people on board to plug gaps that you may have also effectively prevents this from being a challenge for your business.

7. *Failure to adapt to changes and developments:* Continued market research and having a clear plan will help you deal with this scenario.

8. *Unrealistic expectations:* The research and number crunching you undertake in Steps 1 and 2 will help you to effectively remedy any issue regarding unrealistic expectations, further assisted by having a clear business plan.

9. *Poor financial management:* You can deal with this issue by understanding the numbers of your business, having a clear plan, having the right people on board and having the proper systems in place.

10. *Poor administration and record-keeping:* Having the proper systems in place will help you to prevent this issue from arising in your business.

The people you should talk to before you start

Here are some people you should consult before embarking on your journey, mostly because you need to...:

- Your spouse / partner
- Potential business partner(s)
- Potential investors
- Bank manager
- People who have experience of your target market
- Anyone else you can think of who can provide feedback and/or support

How to make your business finally happen

Starting your own business isn't actually that difficult. It is challenging, without a doubt, but now that you've gone through the book hopefully you know that it is a lot less challenging than you might have originally imagined.

The biggest challenge is actually you, or rather, your fears.

You have the knowledge you need - the next step is to take action. That is the only way you'll ever make this happen. That is the only way your business idea will see the light of day.

Just push through your fears and get started. Follow the steps - they will cut down your risks massively. Keep working at it, and follow through.

There's no reason you can't have your own business up and running in a month from now, if not less.

All you need to do is take action.

Last words

Starting your own business will take work, but the steps and sequence laid out so far will, hopefully, help simplify the process for you.

One of my main goals for this book has been to cut down on stuff that isn't absolutely necessary, and make it as actionable as possible. In this day and age, information overload is one of our biggest challenges - and I don't want you to get overwhelmed. As Ralph Waldo Emerson said, "There are many things of which a wise man might wish to be ignorant".

You don't need to know it all (don't even try to, it's futile). You only need to know enough to do what you need to do. So don't stop yourself from starting your business only because you think you don't know everything. Figure out the things you absolutely need to know, and once you have that body of knowledge you know enough.

This book will give you the information you absolutely need to get your business going.

Just follow the steps, and you should be well on your way.

You can always learn more later.

On that point, check out the resource website for additional resources, guides and bonus content.
www.BusinessLaunchCode.com

Creating a successful business takes work, and time; it won't happen overnight. That's why I stressed the importance of perseverance and patience in the beginning. It will be quite a ride, and there will be ups and downs, but it will all be worth it - if you just stick with it.

Now go start your journey!

Further Reading

These are 10 of the best books to read for anyone who wants to start their own business.

The information in this book should be enough for you to start your business - the additional reading is just that, additional reading. Saying that, do check them out once you're up and running as they can provide useful insights and ideas.

- *The Purple Cow* by Seth Godin (great book about being unique - must read for every entrepreneur)
- *Freesourcing* by Jonathen Yates (if you want to know how to start/run a business with little to no money, read this)
- *The 4-Hour Workweek* by Tim Ferriss (this will revolutionise the way you run business!)
- *The $100 Startup* by Chris Guillebeau (another great book on starting and running a business on little to no money)
- *The Lean Startup* by Eric Ries (useful read on how to make your business lean, and effective)
- *The 7 Habits of Highly Effective People* by Stephen Covey (one of the best books for entrepreneurs, on

effective habits)

- *Ready, Fire, Aim* by Michael Masterson (great book on the stages of business, and what it takes to move up)

- *The Snowball* by Alive Shroeder (autobiography of Warren Buffet - useful for learning what it takes to create something spectacular)

- *Steve Jobs* by Walter Isaacson (autobiography of Steve Jobs - love him or hate him, you can learn a lot from this about business)

- *The Real Deal* by James Caan (biography of James Caan - insightful read about an entrepreneur's journey)

If this book has been helpful

The main reason for writing this book is to help as many people as possible. So it is always good to hear from anyone who has found this useful.

On that note, if you found the information in this book valuable, please consider leaving a review - reviews help the book reach other readers who can benefit from it.

Also, please spread the word - if you know anyone who this book can help, do let them know. The more people it can reach, the more it can help. Use the hashtag #BusinessLaunchCode to share your stories, ideas and suggestions.

Pay it forward!

PS. As a thank you for your help, and for being on this journey with me, there are some additional resources (workbook, worksheets, etc) which you can download at BusinessLaunchCode.com

Look for the Secret page (password: entrepreneur).

Acknowledgements

Thanks to all the people who saw me through the book: to all those who provided support, read, wrote, offered comments, and helped in the editing, proofreading, and design.

In particular, a big thanks goes to my wife - without her nudging me to get the book out there (and editorial advice) it probably would have stayed in my virtual-storage a few more years!

There are several others whose help has been invaluable, in particular: Wendy, Fabliha, Omy, Lali, Paula, Shel - I can't thank them enough.

Special thanks also go out to all the authors and entrepreneurs who've helped me gain the experiences and knowledge that made writing this book possible.

Last and not least: I beg forgiveness of all those who have been with me over the course of the years and whose names I have failed to mention.

Disclaimer

All the material contained in this book is provided for educational and informational purposes only. The author, his agents, heirs, and assignees do not accept any responsibilities for any liabilities, actual or alleged, resulting from the use of this information. No responsibility can be taken for any results or outcomes resulting from the use of this material. This book is not "professional advice." The author encourages the reader to seek advice from a professional where any reasonably prudent person would do so.

While every attempt has been made to provide information that is both accurate and effective, the author and his affiliates cannot assume any responsibility for errors, inaccuracies or omissions, including omissions in transmission or reproduction. Any references to people, events, organizations, or business entities are for educational and illustrative purposes only, and no intent to falsely characterise, recommend, disparage, or injure is intended or should be so construed. Any results stated or implied are consistent with general results, but this means results can and will vary. The author, his agents, and assigns, make no promises or guarantees, stated or implied. Individual results will vary and this work is supplied strictly on an "at your own risk" basis.

Dedications

To Mum & Mia,
you guys make my world better.

Also, to all future entrepreneurs,
and the lives they will transform.

About the Author

M Salek FRSA is an award-winning philanthropist, author, business strategist and entrepreneur. He's the founder and CEO of Business Lab, a business strategy consultancy focused on helping businesses grow and improve. With over a decade's experience in business, he has helped start and grow multiple successful businesses from scratch, as well as advised and mentored numerous more.

One of UK's first Certified Business Mentor, Salek is passionate about helping others and making a positive difference in the world.

When not working on his next project, he can be found learning new things, relaxing with gardening, obsessing over food or travelling the world.

For suggestions and feedback, he can be reached at feedback@businesslaunchcode.com

Find out more:
- Website: mhasalek.com
- LinkedIn: linkedin.com/in/msalek
- Twitter: twitter.com/mhasalek

www.ingramcontent.com/pod-product-compliance
Lightning Source LLC
Chambersburg PA
CBHW022046190326
41520CB00008B/720